More Magic

Paul Daniels oftconjurer or, indeed, a magic  d more. He prefers to be calconjures' up magical mysterie up his own style of comedy a

In a matter o  umber one magician (funjurer) in Britain and is gradually becoming internationally known as a 'sparkling entertainer' with a glowing personality.

The wide variety of magic which he presents so expertly on his own television programmes and stage shows, has achieved him much fame and distinction.

Here, in his second book of magic, Paul Daniels discloses some of his secrets together with solid professional advice for young magicians on how to perform magic tricks properly and entertainingly.

Whilst he is known as a 'funny man', Paul takes his profession very seriously. He simply hates seeing tricks and illusions performed badly – even by some of the top magicians!

He offers his readers some of the most entertaining tricks and mysteries ever seen. Many have been specially devised for his books and Paul's own touch of originality shines through.

Treat his magic and secrets with loving care – they will serve you well. Whenever you wish to entertain small groups at home, larger groups at school, or even larger crowds at concerts and local fêtes, his magic will always make their eyes pop out!

But please remember Paul's 'Password' – *Keep the secrets secret, or they won't be secret any more!*

Also by Paul Daniels
in Piccolo

Paul Daniels Magic Book

Paul Daniels

More Magic

Illustrated by Roger Walker

Scholastic Publications Ltd
in association with **Pan Books**

First published in Great Britain 1981 by Pan Books Ltd,
Cavaye Place, London SW10 9PG
Scholastic Publications edition published 1981
© Paul Daniels 1981
Illustrations © Roger Walker 1981
ISBN 0 330 26627 6
Made and printed in Great Britain by
Hunt Barnard Printing Ltd., Aylesbury, Bucks.

Contents

Introduction — Here's More Magic!

I cannot tell you how 'onoured and 'umbled I am to have been asked to write another book on magic for you, and I hope that you enjoy the magic in this book just as much as you apparently enjoyed the magic in the first book (otherwise I wouldn't have been asked to write this one, would I?).

In the first book I explained to you that I thought magic should be fun, and I really believe this. If you are not enjoying what you are doing on the stage – or at your party – you can't expect the audience to enjoy it, and one of the best ways to enjoy magic is to make sure that you are doing it properly. If you do not have to worry about the actual 'mechanics' of the trick you will be a lot more relaxed in your presentation. Therefore, *please, please, please* rehearse all the tricks very carefully and completely before showing them to ANYONE AT ALL.

I am not going to repeat the rules that I stated in the first book in a block because I know some of you already know them. But if you look through the pages of this book, as you learn the tricks, you will find those rules boxed with little stars like this ★★. Don't ignore these rules, they are very very important.

Another thing that became apparent after the first book was published was that you – the new breed of funjurors – wanted tricks that were a little more difficult, a little larger, a little more professional and, therefore, this book is a little more serious in its approach to magic. However, it is really more serious only because I want you to learn it properly, and I repeat that, when performing, try to have a lot of fun and make your magic as entertaining as possible. That is the real magic of show business, it is called entertainment!

PAUL DANIELS

Funny Lines and Patter

When I was very young (what a memory!) I was not funny either on or off stage — I performed what is known as a 'silent' act. This means that the performer does not say anything at all but does his act to music.

This style may suit you too, but if you have a feeling that you would like to be a funny man, or woman, on stage then what I did may be of interest, and use, to you.

I LEARNED to be funny by reading every joke book I could lay my hands on, by listening to radio and TV comedians, and by tape-recording my own magic shows to see if I could spot what made people laugh.

Then, I NEVER told a joke, or said a funny line, that wasn't related to what I was doing, or what I had on stage to perform with. I know rules can be broken but GENERALLY it doesn't make sense to stop in the middle of a trick, or between tricks, and tell a joke that has nothing at all to do with your act!

Here's a selection of lines I have found to be funny when used in the right place in my act. Don't use my exact words though — say them in your own way and with your own timing.

Hold out your hand — no, the clean one! (Comedy is strange — you can reverse the 'joke' and it will still be funny — see how the next line makes fun of a very clean hand.)

My goodness that's a good hand – have you had it dry cleaned?

Now don't argue – remember I'm the one who's clever here!

What's your name? 'Susan' – Why that was my name when I was a girl!

If you think that was clever you should see me when there's a full moon.

(When picking up a wand.) You have heard of the Mystic East? – Well this is 'me stick'. (Lines like this MUST be delivered with a tongue-in-cheek attitude or the audience will lynch you!)

This trick leaves audiences so baffled they sometimes don't start clapping until the end of the next act.

Good ladies, evening and gentlemen . . .

Hello, my name is Paul Daniels – how's that for a memory feat?

Hello, my name is Paul Daniels – I expect you can remember yours just as well . . .

Mispronounce a word when you pick an object up – for example call a handkerchief a 'hunkerchuff' – the audience will yell at you to correct you. Repeat 'hunkerchuff' a couple of times and they'll go bananas to put you right. Finally say 'Oh that's no good, I can't say handkerchief' and go straight on – it drives audiences wild!

1 *The Disappearing Inch of Space*

The props you will need for this trick:
A square of cardboard 8 inches by 8 inches (20 centimetres by 20 centimetres)

Here is a great trick to take to school to show to your Math's Master and with a little bit of luck it will probably confound him.

You can make it in cardboard, or thin plywood, or, if you are very, very clever, thin sheet plastic. You need a square of material 8 inches by 8 inches (20 by 20 centimetres). Cut along the lines as shown in drawing No 1 and once they are cut reassemble the pieces to form a rectangle as shown in drawing No 2. As you can see – and you can

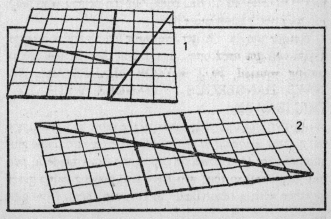

even mark it along the sides of the pieces – the area of this rectangle is now 13 inches by 5 inches (32.5 by 12.5 centimetres), and that makes a total of 65 square inches (162.5 sq centimetres). You started off with an area 8 inches by 8 inches (20 by 20 centimetres) which is 64 square inches (160 sq centimetres). Where did the extra inch come from, and where on earth did it go to?

2 Reds and Blacks

The props you will need for this trick:
5 razor blades, glue, cards, envelopes and a magnet

You will probably need the help of a male adult who shaves in order to do this trick, but the person who helps you may never know quite how.

You see you have to get five razor blades and it is better if you can get used ones. There will then be less risk of cutting yourself, BUT RAZOR BLADES ARE ALWAYS DANGEROUS – HANDLE WITH EXTREME CARE.

Lay five black playing cards on the table face down and put a razor blade on to the middle of each card. Now glue another card face down on top of the razor blade in perfect alignment so that you have two playing cards glued together with a razor blade in between them. Now glue extra cards to the back of five red playing cards so that in outward appearance they seem to be of the same construction as the black ones. They do not, however, have a razor blade between, and this enables you to perform a really good trick.

Hand out the red and the black cards and some small envelopes into which the cards will just fit. Have the envelopes shuffled and the cards shuffled and then passed among the audience so that a lot of different people get to put a card into each envelope. Then the cards, sealed in the envelopes, are shuffled again and you collect them all up.

Putting them behind your back you separate them into two piles with five envelopes in each pile, and when the envelopes are opened it is found that you have separated the red cards from the black ones.

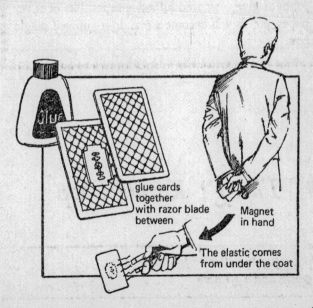

glue cards together with razor blade between

Magnet in hand

The elastic comes from under the coat

How? It is very easy. Hanging just underneath the back of your coat you have a small magnet and the magnet will tell you which envelopes have a black card in because the razor blade will be attracted to the magnet even through the card and through the envelope. Those that are not attracted must have red cards inside. Keep the cards in their envelopes very close to your back so that people cannot see you feeling for the strength of the magnet against your back.

Wisdom Box 1

★★★
Many magicians keep a box of 'off-cuts' of decorative plastic and paper that they can stick on to their props when they are making them up.

It is useful if this box also contains bottles and tubes of glue, coloured adhesive tapes, bits of silver paper, etc. It will become a real do-it-yourself magic box.
★★★

3 *The £1 Karate Chop*

The props you will need for this trick:
A pencil and a £1 note

It is very important that as a Magician you should be able to do tricks with any object at any time, and remembering this trick and how to do it will help you to achieve that kind of reputation.

Have someone hold the ends of a pencil *very tightly*, and make sure it is a long pencil. Then you take the £1 note and fold it along its length and then show that your hands are empty before, and after, the trick.

When you go to do it you must bring your hand down three times – clenching the folded £1 note at one end with your fist. This counting should be done briskly, but quite smoothly, counting 1 – 2 – 3. As you come down very hard on the count of 3 extend your right forefinger and it will break the pencil in its centre provided you carry on right down through the pencil, immediately returning your finger into your fist. It will look as though you have chopped through the pencil with the £1 note. As the person who is holding the pencil ends will be facing you directly try turning the £1 note at a slight angle to

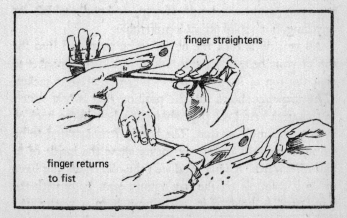

finger straightens

finger returns to fist

your right and this will conceal your finger – extending and returning – from his view, although the third 'chop' should be done so quickly no one could see it anyway!

4 Paper Bag Production

The prop you will need for this trick:
A flat paper bag

This is a very good opening trick because the production is quite startling.

You start off holding a folded flat paper bag in your hand which you unfold and, reaching inside the paper bag, you produce a bottle of pop, or handkerchiefs, or anything, but a solid object is preferable.

All you do is tuck the object to be produced into the top of your belt, or have it lodged in a special pocket so that the top of it comes just to the edge of your jacket. (The drawing shows you the position that is best suited to this trick.) And the paper bag has a hole in the back of it. It is as simple as that. The bag is demonstrated to be empty because it is flat, you never show the inside of it, and afterwards, having produced the object, all you have to do is crumple up the bag against your body with the hand that is holding it, and dump it in a wastepaper

a hole is
cut in bag

basket. Remember to retrieve it later, however, because some people *do* tend to go through thrown away props to see if they can see how the trick was done.

5 *A Loopy Loop Trick*

The props you will need for this trick:
Loops of paper, scissors and glue

The Magician gives a loop of paper to each of two spectators and keeps one for himself, and then hands out pairs of scissors to cut the loops into two. The Magician shows them how to do it by cutting along the middle of the length of the strip of paper, and he finishes up with two loops of the same size. The first spectator tries to cut along the same route that the Magician took, and finds himself with two loops of paper but they are inter-linked and cannot be separated without tearing the paper.

The second person who tries it finds himself with one loop but it is twice as big as the loop he started out with.

To perform this trick all you need are some long strips of paper about 2 inches (5 centimetres) wide. When you stick them into a loop shape by joining the ends, make sure that the first strip of paper is absolutely straight on the loop that you are going to cut. On the next strip of paper give the paper a single twist and on the last one a full twist by turning the paper over and then over again before sticking it. The drawings will make this very clear to you. Then, when you cut along the dotted line shown in the diagram, the trick will work as I have described.

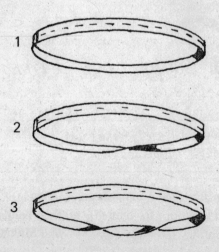

★★

Never tell the audience, or even one person, how a trick is done. It will not make them appreciate the time you have spent learning to entertain with that trick. They will just think it was very simple and credit you with no skill at all.

★★

6 *The Hypnotized Arm*

The props you will need for this trick:
A friend with an arm

Although this trick is not done by hypnosis you tell a friend that you are going to hypnotize his arm, but he has to obey your commands.

Stand him very close to a wall with his right side next to the wall and his right wrist actually touching the wall. He has to push outwards with his arm but not his body, as if he is trying to push the wall away from him. He has to really *try* to push the wall away from himself. He must not let his body come away from the wall, nor must he let his body touch his wrist which is pushing outwards against the wall. You keep commanding his arm to push against the wall for about thirty seconds. He must press hard. Then you tell him to step away from the wall and let his arm hang by his side. You command his arm to float away (he must not try to stop it, but just to let it go and let his arm hang down) and his arm *will* float away! It will rise away from his body giving your friend quite a peculiar feeling.

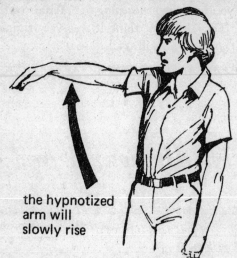

the hypnotized
arm will
slowly rise

7 *Egg Production*

The props you will need for this trick:
Hat or box, handkerchief, eggs and egg box, long needle, thread, glue, cotton, a chair, material, tent poles and a plastic box for eggs

---

This trick is a real oldie – but don't let that put you off. The funny thing about magic is that, unlike other arts, it doesn't 'date'.

If you were to vanish a pebble today it would be just as baffling as it was 2000 years ago, or 2000 years into the future. Magic is timeless and works just as well in any country in the world – so haven't *you* joined a good club!

Anyway, back to the trick. You show a hat or a box to be empty, and place it on a table – or a chair if you are not very tall. Then you show a large handkerchief and by folding it in half you start to produce eggs, one at a time, by tipping them from the handkerchief into the hat. At the end of the trick you can either produce, say, six eggs IN A BOX, or you can make them disappear again.

It's fun to do, and it is fun to make so let's get on with it.

The first part of the trick is VERY messy – I told you it was fun! You have to blow an egg, and if you have never done it before – OH WOW!

You have to make a small hole at one end of the egg by using a pin – get your hands well into a big bowl or the sink.

Now make a slightly larger hole at the other end and then insert a long needle to break the yolk by wiggling it around – the needle, not the yolk!

Remove the needle, put your lips to the small hole and blow *(Don't suck – it's really yukky)*, the contents of the egg should go into the bowl.

When you have got most of it out put the egg into a bowl of water, large hole uppermost, and the water will fill the egg – swish it around, blow it out, and keep doing it until the water comes out clean. Blow it all out, dry it completely – it shouldn't take too long.

Now you have to sew an egg – don't worry, the hardest part is threading the needle.

A LONG needle is required because when it is

threaded it has to go in the large hole and out the small hole of the egg, pulling the cotton through with it, of course. Tie a knot in the cotton big enough to go through the large hole but not through the small hole. I also add a blob of glue so that the knot will not untie itself and it also glues it to the inside of the shell.

Now fix the thread to the handkerchief as shown in drawing No 1 so that the egg hangs just below the centre of the handkerchief when corners A and B are held up. It helps if the handkerchief is coloured, and preferably has a pattern.

I know that there has been a lot of work for you already but think about this : I wouldn't ask you to do it if I didn't think the effect was worth it, and if you take a bit of trouble to *make* a trick, you'll have something not many people can be bothered with.

Let's deal with the production of the single eggs first : Don't make a big deal out of the handkerchief – certainly don't pick it up as if it was full of eggs! Just pick it up by holding both corners A and B between the fingers of your left hand (drawing No 2). The egg will hang inside the folds of the handkerchief and the right hand takes hold of corners C and D as in drawing No 3.

The handkerchief is tipped and the egg will be seen to roll out of the hanky and into the hat BUT you must hold the hanky high enough to let the audience see the egg fall across the gap between the bottom of the hanky and the top of the hat. It must also be high enough for the egg not to hit the bottom of the hat!

Immediately the egg has 'fallen', lower the hanky and the left hand takes hold of C as it releases A and B and the handkerchief is straightened, drop C and D FORWARD of the hat with A and B across the brim.

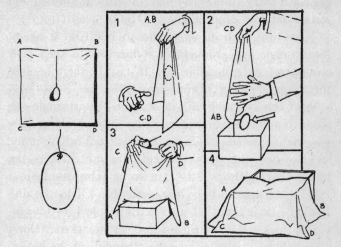

From start to finish all these moves must be done smoothly, evenly and casually – as if producing eggs out of handkerchiefs was the most natural thing in the world. This set of moves is known as the 'single egg production' in what follows.

Remember that you do not need a hat – a box of a similar size will do nicely. The props are laid out so that you can pick them up easily, especially the hanky.

'Ladies and gentlemen, what you are about to see is un-believable. I am going to use this very believable hat (pick it up) which as you can see is empty (put it down). I am going to use this very believable handkerchief (pick it up) –the unbelievable part of the trick is the hen that lives inside the hanky. (Start the single egg production.) It doesn't look big enough to contain a hen, but where else could the egg have come from?' (By now the trick is finished and you should have dropped C and D on the word 'from'.)

'That was such an *egg*cellent trick I'll do it again. (Start single egg production.) Remember to keep your eyes open for the invisible hen. It must be there because there is another egg! (Drop hanky!)

'Isn't this *egg*citing? I'll do it again! (Start single egg production but this time spread your fingers wide to show your hands are empty.) Some people do not believe in the invisible hen, they think the eggs are concealed in the hands – (as egg drops) – they are wrong. (Drop hanky.)

'This hen appears to be in*egg*shaustible. I'll do it again. (Go on – do it again!) I used to tell people I used an invisible duck – it drove them (drop egg) quackers. (Don't drop hanky – casually show the other side of the hanky, go back to original side and then drop it as before.) Show both hands empty and pick the hanky straight up again and do the single egg production *again* as you say:

'Some people find this trick very boring – some find it *hen*tertaining but the yolks, sorry, jokes are *egg*scrutiating.' (Drop hanky on *hen*tertaining.)

Do single egg production one last time as you say: 'So there we have an unbelievable trick with an unbelievable hen, and pretty unbelievable jokes . . .' (By now the hanky should have been dropped as before, but now you pick up the hanky where the thread is sewn into the hem, the egg will be picked up hanging inside the folds, and you lay it to one side, put it in another box or whatever. This *must* be done casually as if you are merely discarding a useless prop. NEVER look at it because an audience will always follow your eyes.) ' . . . and the sad part of magic is that if you don't believe (pick up hat) – it never happens.' (Show hat empty and bow.)

An alternative ending is to produce the eggs at the end and say : 'Now I know you don't believe in the invisible hen, and that doesn't surprise me, and I *know* you probably don't believe in the eggs either, and *that* doesn't surprise me. What surprises *me* is how they got into this box.' (Remove box from hat and quickly open it to show the eggs.)

Now you are probably going to wonder how you get the box of eggs into the empty hat or box, and so am I !

One way would be to make a magic utility chair, and that is the next item in the book – what a coincidence . . .

A utility prop is anything that the Magician can use for several tricks, each effect can be completely different in the presentation, and the prop therefore is *very* useful indeed.

Just about any dining-room type chair can be used or adapted, and I shall cover most of them for you. Let us suppose that you can get your hands on an old Bentwood chair, as shown in the drawing.

It doesn't matter whether you are doing a show in the living-room or whether you are doing a show on a stage. This chair can be faked in a very cunning way to give you a secret space that the audience will never notice. You fill in the space in the hoop of the back of the chair with the same kind of material as the curtaining behind where you are working. To the audience it looks as though they can see straight through the back of the chair to the curtain behind, but on the back of the chair you can fix a box, or a shelf or a hook with something hanging from it, and they can't see it because it is behind your extra piece of material. This is probably the most deceptive of the 'magical' chairs providing you can match the back-cloth

and because it is so very deceptive some magicians carry
around with them their own backdrops which consist of a
frame made of poles rather like their tent poles as shown in
the drawing. They stretch their own material, or hang it
from the top cross rod on this frame and the chair standing in front looks perfectly normal. It also helps if the
chair is painted white; and although this is not necessary,
it does help to catch the eye and draw it to the wood
framework of the chair. Some modern dining chairs have
a solid panel on the back anyway, and although they are
very good and can of course be used just as well, they are
not as magically deceptive as an open backed chair.

One of the uses of such a chair has already been shown
in the preceding trick where you want to produce a box
of eggs inside a hat. Going back to the start of that egg
production trick : have the handkerchief bundled on the
chair with the point where the thread joins the hem of the

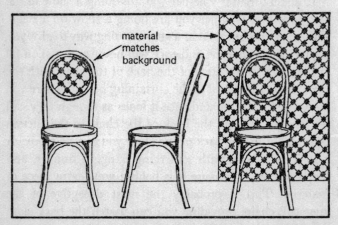

material
matches
background

handkerchief slightly raised, and the egg folded within the folds of the bundle. That hat is placed brim downwards over this pile, and then you pick up the hat and show it empty, as instructed, BUT then you transfer the hat into one hand so that it is held by the brim with the fingers inside and the thumb on the outside. That hand would then rest on the back of the chair as you bend over to pick up the handkerchief from the chair by its raised hem. Now as you lift the handkerchief from the chair you lift the hat away from the back of the chair at the same time, but unknown to the audience your fingers have picked up a loop on which is hanging the box of eggs and it ends up inside the hat.

Until you need them the box of eggs can either be hanging on a hook at the back of the chair, or can be standing on a ledge on the back of the chair. It is possible to buy in hardware stores a little plastic box for eggs that has a handle on one side, and that is perfect for the job because your fingers can easily slip into the handle and swing the box inside the hat as you pick it up. The action of lifting the handkerchief covers the action of picking up the eggs. This can apply to all 'loading' of props from the back of the chair, always do it under cover of some other action.

If you have two chairs that match in shape I would suggest that you do not fill in the back of one of them, and at some time you can then walk behind the unfaked chair and by visual suggestion you have hinted that you could walk behind both of them. NEVER EVER walk behind the chair that is faked otherwise there is no point in going to the trouble of faking it.

★★★

Always be as smart as you can when you perform in public and have your props laid out neatly and tidily. This will give you an appearance of confidence in what you are going to do. Remember an audience does not like an act that appears nervous.

★★★

8 *The Vanishing Pencil*

The props you will need for this trick:
A pencil (with rubber), ball pen, thin round elastic, glue, safety pin

---

The Magician removes from his pocket a pencil and points out that for the pencil to be this length, the lead must be the same distance from the rubber as the rubber is from the lead. He then holds it with two hands, and with some happy little witticism like 'you can take a horse to water but a pencil must be lead' he throws it into the air. Only somehow it never gets quite that far because it seems to have disappeared completely.

How to do it is comparatively simple. You need the top from a cheap ball-pen (you may have to remove the clip) and then you will have to drill a hole in the point. You thread a piece of elastic, preferably the round kind, through the cap and tie a big knot in one end of the elastic so that it won't pull all the way through. A blob of glue on the knot will prevent it untying. The other end of the elastic is fastened to a safety pin and the safety pin is pinned inside your jacket so that when the pencil is inside the cap it will not hang below the level of your jacket. Somewhere in the region of the inside rear shoulder is usually about best. See the drawing for the arrangement.

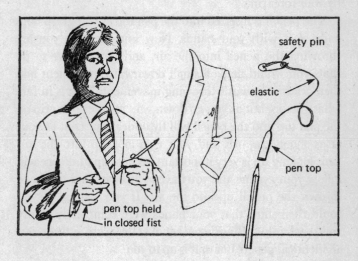

safety pin

elastic

pen top

pen top held in closed fist

Sometimes you cannot easily buy strong elastic, but you can plait three pieces of weak elastic into a very strong 'rope'.

When you go to find the pencil you do not find it straight away, you go through several pockets looking for a pencil. In reality what you are doing is covering the fact that you are pulling the cap round the body and into your right hand. In some instances your right hand can reach

29

into an inside pocket or a rear pocket and obtain the cap itself quite secretly. The left hand brings out the pencil and the right hand points to the lead and the rubber in turn as you explain about the length of the pencil. This pointing covers the fact that your right hand is clenched around the pen top. Your fist should not be clenched too tightly, just a relaxed pointing, with the little finger gripping the pen-top and the elastic which should run out from under your coat but be concealed from the audience by your forearm.

The pencil is inserted into the pen top as you grasp both ends of it with your hands. Now imagine that you are throwing the pencil into the air, and if you were to do that, you would make a small downward movement and then a large upwards throwing movement. This is in fact what you do, but as you go down, you release your grip on the pen top and the pencil will fly under your coat as your arms shoot upwards and your eyes look up into the air. This looking up is very important because an audience will follow your eyeline and you have to 'believe' that you have thrown the pencil up into the air. If you wanted to you could then show that your hands were completely empty and reach into the inside pocket of your jacket and remove an identical pencil, but that is up to you.

Performed briskly and without fumbling this is a real fooler of a trick that can be done when you are completely surrounded and very close to your audience indeed. So it is a good one to do at school, in the playground, as well as on a stage.

9 *The Travelling Coin*

The props you will need for this trick:
A coin (10p), handkerchief, glass of water, plate, small cardboard box, ball of thick chunky wool, brandy glass or jug

---

What you are about to learn is more than just a trick. It is a routine, and I recommend this trick very highly for the concert platform or stage shows.

When you are very familiar with it you will then be able to move a little closer to people with it, and I personally would be prepared to do this trick in a living-room where the people are really quite close to me.

You borrow a silver coin which is then marked so that later it can be verified as being the same coin at the end of the trick. You ask a spectator to hold the coin underneath a handkerchief and drop it into a glass of water. Everyone can hear the plop as it goes into the water and you point out that in olden days Magicians used to do a trick like this where the coin disappeared. This is not the trick that you are about to do you say and you remove the handkerchief from the top of the glass, and there under water is the coin.

The spectator who dropped the coin into the water is now given a plate to place on top of the glass, and he has to stand guard over that to make sure the coin cannot get out.

On the other side of the stage you point out that you

31

have a small cardboard box, and you pick it up and show all four sides of the box and then you remove the lid. Tipping the box upside down you reach inside and pull out a ball of wool that fills the cardboard box. You drop the ball of wool into a large brandy glass, or glass jug, and start to pull out one end of the wool to unravel the ball. The ball of wool will twist and turn inside the glass but its weight should hold it there and when you have the ball of wool almost unwound you ask the spectator to lift the plate from the top of the glass and look inside. He sees nothing at all; if you have timed it correctly, at the same time a coin should fall into the jar or glass out of the ball of wool. You then pick up the glass and tip the coin into the spectator's hand where he verifies that it is the marked coin that he first lent you.

To do this trick you have to pull together quite a few

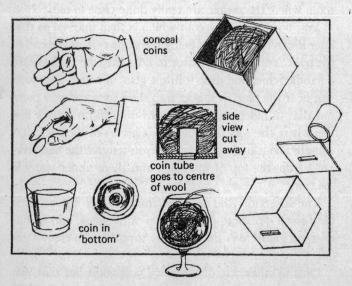

conceal coins

side view cut away

coin tube goes to centre of wool

coin in 'bottom'

props, but I am going to explain each of them to you, and you will find that none of them are very difficult to obtain or make.

First, let us consider the coin that vanishes from the glass. Try this little experiment. Get a glass tumbler, fill it three quarters full with water, and put a coin underneath it. If you look down into the water you can see the coin apparently in the bottom of the water but really it is underneath the glass. Now put a plate on top of the glass and look in through the sides. The coin cannot be seen. You can try this and perform this part of the trick as a magical effect in its own right, but a lot of people know about this kind of thing now that they study light refraction at school.

Find out whether a 10p piece, or a 5p piece, or a 50p piece is the best kind of coin for you to conceal in your hand, and then go to a glaziers and ask him to cut you a piece of glass the same size as the coin. He will probably be bursting with curiosity to know what you want it for, but just explain to him that you are a Magician and you'd rather not tell him. The glass should cost only a few pence if he charges you at all, but do ask him to smooth the edges of the glass off so that you don't cut yourself.

That now explains what you need for the first part of the trick.

By the time you have the coin marked with a pencil or a nail file you should already have the glass disc in the finger palm position. The diagram shows you where this is in your hand, but you should not have your hand closed tightly because this is a dead give away that you are holding something in it. The slightest closing of the fingers will grip the glass disc. When your hand is covered by the handkerchief to offer the spectator his coin through the handkerchief, you swop the glass disc for the coin. Do this without letting them clink together, and once he has grasped the disc through the handkerchief finger palm the coin.

Pick up the glass of water with your other hand and, as it goes underneath the handkerchief for him to drop in the disc (which he believes is the coin), put it on top of the coin that is finger palmed. After the audience have heard the plop, remove the handkerchief and ask him to look down into the glass to check that the coin is there. You do this in a very subtle way. In fact you do not ask him whether the coin is there, you tell him it is by pointing to it and saying 'there is your coin inside the glass and I am going to put this plate on top of it.' You let him see the coin but you do not give him time to think about it.

You place the plate on top of the glass and immediately pick the glass up – with the plate on top of it – with the hand that is *not* holding the coin, and transfer it on to the table next to him. By rotating your hand with the coin finger palmed so that the back of the hand is towards the audience and just letting it fall naturally to the side he won't see it go, because the plate is between him and the coin, and he will be more interested in watching what you're doing with the plate and the glass. You put *that* as close to his body as you can on the table so that he is looking down directly on to the plate and will not notice that the coin has gone yet.

Now, the box with the ball of wool in it is not as simple as it may seem. The way that you make the box is shown very clearly in the drawings but let me give you more advice on its construction. You need to beg, borrow, buy or make a small square box. Cut a square of cardboard that will fit *tightly* into the bottom of the box and in the middle of the square cut a slot big enough for the coin to go through. Make a flat tube of tin or strong card and mount it upright on the slot so that the coin drops through it easily. Cut a slot in the bottom of the box to match the slot in the card.

Wrap the wool – thick wool is best – around the tube as if you were winding a ball and then push it into the box, taking care to line up the slots. As you cross the stage to where the box is situated you must endeavour to bring the coin from a flat finger palm position to a position where it is standing upright and gripped between your second and third fingers. When you pick up the box and place it on your hand it will fit into the slot that is in the bottom of the box.

If on the way across the stage you have pointed out the box and said that this is the second part of the trick, the audience will not notice your hand manoeuvring the coin into position; when you pick up the box and place it on the outstretched palm and fingers of the hand the coin will easily go into the bottom. Watch the angles of your hand at all times so that the audience will not be aware of the coin going in the bottom. Lift the lid and show that the ball of wool fills the box. As you tip it upside down, the coin will slide down the chute that you have made inside the box that goes right to the heart of the wool and you pull the wool off the chute out of the box and squeeze the wool as you do so, it will close the slight gap left by the chute.

Drop the wool into the brandy glass and get ready for the applause.

10 *Who's a Little Smartie, Then?*

The props you will need for this trick:
Smarties in a tube or box, a saucer or small bowl

What a good trick this is. Not only because it is amazing, not only because it is baffling, but because you get to eat the Smarties! To be honest you could use jelly babies or any other coloured sweets for this trick once you understand the principle.

If you open a tube or a packet of Smarties you will find that there are lots of different colours, and for this trick you select six of them. In order to explain the trick to you I am going to use red, green, purple, yellow, brown and orange, and I lay one of each of those colours out in a row in that order. As I am standing behind the table with the Smarties on it, the red one is to the left, then the green, then the purple, the yellow is in the number 4 position from the left, then the brown and then the orange. The position of the yellow Smartie is very important because I have removed *all* the yellow Smarties from the tube, and left a mixture of all the other colours. As I don't need the rest of the yellow ones, I've eaten them which adds to my enjoyment of the trick anyway. Stand the tube on the table next to the displayed row of Smarties and you are all ready to go.

Use introductory lines like 'For this next trick I've become a bit of a Smartie-pants' and they'll probably throw you out!

Quite simply what the audience does is to choose a number from 1 to 6 and when the tube is opened and tipped into a saucer, or a small bowl, the audience can see that the colour of that number is the very colour that was your favourite and you've eaten all those Smarties before the trick started.

Obviously you have to arrive at the yellow Smartie and you are probably wondering if the audience is given a free

red	green	purple	yellow	brown	orange
⬤	⬤	⬤	⬤	⬤	⬤
			E	N	O
			O	W	T
			3	2	1
1	2	3	4		
F	I	V	E		
			X	I	S

choice how you get there. Well, my friends, once again I am about to teach you how to cheat.

If the audience chooses No 1 you spell the word 'one' starting from the orange Smartie on the right 'o – n – e'. You are spelling backwards but to the audience it will look the right way round. For the No 2 you do exactly the same thing. You spell 't – w – o', of course you will arrive at the yellow Smartie on the letter 'o'. For No 3 you count starting at the orange Smartie '1 – 2 – 3'. For the No 4 you count from the left hand end of the row starting at the red Smartie '1 – 2 – 3 – 4' to the yellow Smartie. For No 5 you start to spell from the red end 'F – i – v – e' arriving at the yellow Smartie on 'e', and for No 6 you spell 's – i – x' from the right hand end. You must learn to do this almost without thinking, so that the moment the number is stated you can immediately carry on saying 'the number chosen is six and we are going to spell that word starting at the orange Smartie, s –i – x, and the Smartie you have chosen is the yellow one, by an amazing coincidence, or is it magic, those are my favourite Smarties and if you look inside the tube and tip them into this dish you will find that those are the only ones I've eaten this morning. Isn't it amazing?'

There is a general rule in magic you must never repeat a trick for the same audience at the same time. Always leave a period of time in which anyone who has seen a trick before will forget the details and, therefore, not notice a repetition of method, or in the case of the Smarties trick, a change in the way you count or spell. This particular trick therefore with the Smarties must *never ever* be repeated for the same audience at the same time, and this rule with this trick must *never ever* be broken.

11   *A Literary Tea Break*

The props you will need for this trick:
A paperback book, a sandwich and orange juice

Visual jokes are quite rare when compared with the number of verbal jokes that you hear around, and when I was very young in magic I remember cutting the middle out of the pages of a book so that I could put a sandwich inside and during the act pick up the book, open it, take out the sandwich, take a bite, put it back in the book, close the book, and this went on throughout the act. Now on paper that doesn't sound like very much but I found that the laughter grew every time I did this repetitive joke. If you look closely at the drawing you will see that I have added an extra to this book idea so that the joke finishes up with a strong tag.

I had better explain what a tag is. It is the little bit at the end of a joke that makes it funny. In a 'story' joke it is sometimes known as the punch line, but in a visual joke you just don't have a line, do you? So it is called a tag. This book *is* very educational, isn't it! Of course it is.

As I have said the construction of the hollow book should be fairly obvious from the drawings, so let me tell you how to handle it. The book must be leaning against a box or another prop on the table so that it doesn't spill. When you have completed a trick pick it up and, holding it upright, open the first few pages, remove the sandwich, let the audience see you take a bite of the sandwich, put it

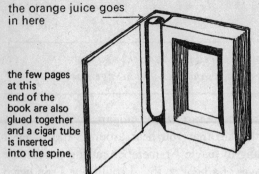

the orange juice goes in here

the book is glued together except for the front few pages — then a hole is cut out of the solid block, slightly bigger than the sandwich.

the few pages at this end of the book are also glued together and a cigar tube is inserted into the spine.

back in the book and stand the book up on the table. Try to develop a 'feeling' for this trick because you may not want to do this biting of the sandwich between every trick although, of course, if your show only has two or three tricks in it you may want to take a bite of the sandwich right in the middle of one of your magical effects, but make sure you don't interfere with the flow of that effect.

When the end of your show comes, pick up the book as if you are going to eat the sandwich again, open it, look at the audience, close it, pick up a glass and quickly pour out the orange juice, say 'cheers', take a drink and then take a bow.

The book must, of course, be a paperback so that you can still open it although the first inch or so is glued together near the spine. Don't cut this book up or you won't remember how to handle the trick after you've made it!

★★
★ Never repeat the same trick for the same audience at ★
★ the same time, whether it be an audience of one or an ★
★ audience of a thousand. ★
★★

12 *Clipped*

The props you will need for this trick:
A £1 note (or paper), paper clips of various sizes,
ribbons or streamers

This particular stunt is useful because you can do it virtually anywhere. You merely fold a pound note into three equal parts and clip it together with two paper clips as shown in the drawing. Pulling the ends of the pound note so that it straightens itself causes the two paper clips to come off the pound note joined together.

From that simple idea can come a lot of entertainment. In the first place you don't even have to use a pound note, of course, you can use any strip of paper. Also you can try concealing a string of smaller paper clips attached to one of the larger paper clips, firstly in your hand and then within the folds of the pound note. Each person I have shown this to tends to handle it in their own way, so I would advise you to work out your method of getting

pull ⬅️   ➡️ pull

them into the right situation. Practise it first with only two or three little paper clips attached to the larger paper clip and you can tell a story of Mr and Mrs Paperclip who got married and had lots of little paper clips. If you want to make it into a more visual stage effect you can buy very large paper clips from a stationers and attach ribbons or paper streamers to the bottom of them. Pulling the ends of the paper taut will cause them to fly into the air and you can catch them. This would make a nice item in a silent act.

13 *Wow!*

The props you will need for this trick:
Cards, ribbons or tape, a box or hat, double-sided sticky
tape (Sellotape)

The ending to this trick can either be very clean and neat, or it can be very messy. It depends entirely upon you and your style of presentation. Certainly using the messy ending to the trick is more showy, but it depends whether you want to crawl around on your hands and knees afterwards picking up a pack of cards. You may, of course, be very rich and just leave the pack of cards lying around and use a fresh pack for every performance!

To the audience it appears that you have a card chosen, returned it to the pack, and then bound the pack round and round with a broad piece of ribbon or tape. Holding the loose end of the tape you throw the pack into the air! The ribbon unwinds, and the cards scatter all over the place, but dangling on the end of the ribbon is the very card that was chosen. Isn't it wonderful? Isn't it messy?

So an alternative presentation is to wrap the cards up in the tape and lower them into a box or a hat. By pulling one end of the tape back out the cards will rotate inside the box and only one card will come out on the end and that is the chosen card again. Either trick is done in exactly the same way and you'll need a pack of cards, a length of ribbon and some double-sided sticky tape like Sellotape.

First you cut a piece of the sticky tape and put it on one end of the ribbon. Lay the ribbon on your magic table or amongst your props in such a way that the tape does not stick to anything, including the table top. Now all you have to do is to have a card chosen and control it so that it comes to the top of the pack. Stick the end of the ribbon on to the back of the top card as you wrap the ribbon round and round the pack, and of course it will be the only one attached to the ribbon when all the rest fall off.

Don't panic about how to get the card into position, I'll tell you how, but of course if you can work out your own method then that pleases me even more because it shows that you are thinking about the magic and not just copying me.

ribbon spread

wow!

All you have to do is shuffle a pack of cards and get the Joker to the bottom of the deck. Ribbon spread the cards across the table top and ask someone to remove one of the cards (see drawing). Ask them to look at it and remember it, and as they are looking at the card and remembering it, you gather the cards up again into a single pile with the Joker still on the bottom. Tell them to replace their card on the top and cut the cards and complete the cut as many times as they want to. Cutting the cards never disturbs the order of a pack, and the Joker will always be on top of the chosen card. Having completed their cuts they then give you the pack back, and you say that you will remove the Joker because he does tend to interfere with the trick. So you look through the pack and cut the Joker back to the bottom of the deck. The chosen card will now be on the top and you can remove the Joker and put it to one side. Show that the bottom card is not the chosen card and by lifting two cards off the top of the pack as if they were only one card (in other words you keep all the edges pressed together) you show that the *top* card is not the chosen card either. You replace the two cards as one on top of the pack and wrap it round with the ribbon, and all the dirty deeds are done. You may now throw the cards in the air and attached to the end of the ribbon will be the chosen card.

That sneaky move of lifting two cards from the top as one must be practised very carefully because it is one of the most useful little bits of card magic. It is known as the double lift and you will find it in many books that specialize in card magic.

Why did I call the trick 'Wow'? Well, that is what the audience will say when they see the card dangling on the end of the ribbon. *Wow!*

14 *An Impossible Ring Trick*

The props you will need for this trick:
A ring, a length of string, sticky tape and a table or cloth

Unfortunately, with so many magic tricks, you have to make the props before you can start your performance. At the very least you must gather the props together that are necessary to make the trick work. With this trick, however, all you need is a length of string and a finger ring. The finger ring should be solid and there is nothing faked about the string. Therefore you should be able to find these items lying around the house.

Your wrists are tied together, as shown in the drawing, the knots can be sealed by wrapping them round with sticky tape and those seals can be examined before and after the trick. You then take the finger ring – in fact this can be any finger ring that is offered to you – put your hands under the table, or underneath a cloth held by two spectators if you are doing this on a stage, and in practically no time at all your hands come back out from under the table with the ring not only on the string but knotted on the string. This is a doddle to do but it is very baffling if you don't know the method.

Once your hands are out of sight under the table or the cloth or wherever, you merely pass a loop of string from between your wrists through the ring and, having got it through the ring, you slip that loop *under* the string tied around your left wrist. Pass it over your left hand, under

the string at the back of the left hand again and pull it away from the hand, and you will then find that the ring is then tied on to the string. Do this under cover of muttering some mysterious incantation such as 'hey diddle diddle we're working a fiddle' and I think that you will find your friends are quite amazed. Not by the trick, but that you are daft enough to say 'hey diddle diddle we're working a fiddle' out loud!

✳✳

Always wash your hands before practising your
magic and certainly before showing it to anyone else.
This will not only improve your appearance (nobody
likes to see dirty finger nails), but it will also keep
your props (cards, ropes, handkerchiefs, etc.) cleaner
longer.

✳✳

15 *For Two Pins . . .*

The props you will need for this trick:
A safety pin and a large cotton handkerchief

Actually this trick has got nothing to do with two pins at
all. I was just stuck for a title and had to call it something
that you could remember it by. In fact you only use one
pin and a cotton handkerchief, preferably a gent's large
size handkerchief, and it is even better if you have bor-
rowed it from someone. I don't have to tell an intelligent
person like yourself to use a clean handkerchief – do I?

To perform the trick lay the handkerchief on a table
and fold it in half so that the fold is nearest to you and the
four corners point away from you. Take a safety pin and
pin the handkerchief by putting the point of the pin
beneath the fold and letting it come up through the hand-

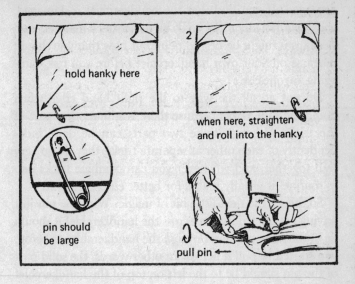

1 hold hanky here

2 when here, straighten
and roll into the hanky

pin should
be large

pull pin ←

kerchief for about $\frac{1}{2}$ inch (1.25 cm), so that the pin is sticking through *both* thicknesses of cloth before you close it back into its cap. If you look closely at the drawing you will see that when it is closed it is laid with the solid part of the pin to the left and the unclippable part of the pin to the right. You will also notice that I have pinned through the handkerchief towards the left hand edge. Now grasp the left hand edge of the handkerchief at the bottom nearest your body and grasp the pin at *its* bottom, and angling it slightly (as shown in the drawing) pull it firmly to the right. It will apparently go through the material, but the material will not be damaged at all – it just slides along. When you get to the other end you must learn to make a slight forward stab to put the pin back through the material. It really looks as though you have torn right across the handkerchief but the handkerchief is un-

49

damaged. If you find that the handkerchief *is* damaged, you have not done the trick in the correct manner, and perhaps it might be best to point out now that you should rehearse on your own handkerchief before you risk damaging anyone else's!

Do not go all the way to the right hand edge when doing the pull across because there is still another part of the trick. Although these two parts can be done independently of each other as separate tricks, they do go very well together, and whenever you can combine tricks into a 'routine' it usually makes for better entertainment.

So, here's the next little bit of magic. With the pin just having completed its run across the handkerchief it should be in the same position *through* the handkerchief as before you started to pull it across. In other words, the solid part of the pin should be to the left on top of the handkerchief and the part that goes through the handkerchief should run underneath and out again and into the clip on the top of the safety pin and be to the right of that pin. Now grasp the bottom of the pin and twist the whole pin to the right. If you do that again the pin will start to roll the handkerchief around it. Do it once or twice, or even three times if you feel in the mood, and then grasp the handkerchief above where the pin lies within its folds. (See drawing.) You must keep a firm hold of the handkerchief and you must grasp the pin with an equally firm grip where it is sticking out at the bottom. Pull the pin out of the folds of the handkerchief confidently and you will find that the pin just comes away leaving the handkerchief again in its undamaged state.

16 *I've Got Your Number*

The props you will need for this trick:
Copies of the 'cards' drawn in the book, coins or counters

If anyone was to ask me which was the most important trick, not only in this book, but in my life, it would have to be the trick that I am about to teach you. The reason is simple, it was the very first trick I ever learned, and from this very small beginning I have built a career of magic that has included cabaret clubs, television series, theatres and even Royal Variety Shows. Who knows, it may do the same for you, but even if it doesn't you will still have a handy pocket-size trick with which to amuse, amaze, baffle and bewilder your friends and relatives.

If you look at the drawing that accompanies this trick you will see six cards covered in numbers, and although they are in numerical order not all the same numbers are on any one card. A volunteer – or it can be somebody you've picked on at random – thinks of a number between 1 and 63 and indicates to you which card or cards show their number. Immediately you can tell them what their number is. I will teach you the method and then I will teach you several improvements. Think of any number now – yourself – between 1 and 63 and place a coin or a counter on the cards in the drawing that have your number on them. Now add up the top left hand numbers on those cards and you will see it adds up to your number. Try it again with a different number. Add up the left hand corners of the cards that the number is on and you will find that they *always* add up to the chosen number. Clever isn't it? This trick is not only entertaining, it is educational – it improves your adding up ability.

So now you know the basic idea you can copy those cards out yourself, or you can have them typed on to blank cards about the size of a playing card, and you can perform the trick immediately in its basic form. It is always nice, however, to improve a trick if you possibly can and here are a couple of suggestions that I have come up with over the years.

One, have the cards set out in order, so that the card with No 1 in the top left hand corner is on the top. Below that is the No 2, then No 4, then No 8, then No 16 and the card with No 32 in the top left hand corner is at the bottom of the pile. Hand them to someone who has thought of a number from 1 to 63 and tell him to gaze at the card and put it in his left hand pocket if it has got his number on, or to put it in his right hand pocket if it has not. All you do is add up the numbers that go into the left hand pocket by remembering which card he is up to in the pile. This sounds a lot more complicated than it really is, because all you have to remember are the numbers 1, 2, 4, 8, 16 and 32. All numbers from 1 to 63 are a combination of these, and you just have to follow very closely which cards are going into which pockets.

Another way is to mark the back of the cards with a secret mark like pencil dots, and before he starts the trick he can shuffle the cards, then look at them and the ones that have his number on he has to hold against his forehead before he places them into his pocket. As he holds them against his forehead you can see the marks and know what is on the front, so you can again add up the basic numbers and arrive at the numbers he thought of.

```
1,  3,  5,  7,  9,  11, 13,
15, 17, 19, 21, 23, 25, 27,
29, 31, 33, 35, 37, 39, 41,
43, 45, 47, 49, 51, 53, 55,
57, 59, 61, 63
```

```
2,  3,  6,  7,  10, 11, 14,
15, 18, 19, 22, 23, 26, 27,
30, 31, 34, 35, 38, 39, 42,
43, 46, 47, 50, 51, 54, 55,
58, 59, 62, 63
```

```
4,  5,  6,  7,  12, 13, 14,
15, 20, 21, 22, 23, 28, 29,
30, 31, 36, 37, 38, 39, 44,
45, 46, 47, 52, 53, 54, 55,
60, 61, 62, 63
```

```
8,  9,  10, 11, 12, 13, 14,
15, 24, 25, 26, 27, 28, 29,
30, 31, 40, 41, 42, 43, 44,
45, 46, 47, 56, 57, 58, 59,
60, 61, 62, 63
```

```
16, 17, 18, 19, 20, 21, 22,
23, 24, 25, 26, 27, 28, 29,
30, 31, 48, 49, 50, 51, 52,
53, 54, 55, 56, 57, 58, 59,
60, 61, 62, 63
```

```
32, 33, 34, 35, 36, 37, 38,
39, 40, 41, 42, 43, 44, 45,
46, 47, 48, 49, 50, 51, 52,
53, 54, 55, 56, 57, 58, 59,
60, 61, 62, 63
```

Yet another way is to have them all on differently coloured cards and then you have to remember which colour goes with which basic number.

Once you have totally mastered this trick you can, of course, do it as a platform or stage effect by standing the person across the stage from yourself, and if you keep your patter and attitude very casual it can appear that you hardly looked at the cards at all, and afterwards people will not, in fact, remember you were paying any attention to what your volunteer was doing. So there you have it, lots of different presentations for the same trick. You, of course, may improve on what I have written for you and come up with your own way of handling this superb effect.

Never think that because a trick is simple it is no good. Very recently I have fooled two top television producers with the trick that you have just learned.

17 *The Three Dice Trick*

The props you will need for this trick:
Three dice, preferably of different colours

This trick is based on a mathematical principle that has been concealed within the presentation. You show three dice and have them rolled several times to prove that they are not faked in any way and that each time a different set of numbers come out on top. Now you turn your back and ask someone to roll the dice and add the three faces on the top together. For example there may be a four, a three and a one, which will give him a total of 8. Now your volunteer has to pick up any one of the dice and add the bottom number – that is the one that has just been resting on the table – to the total of the top faces. Now he has to roll that dice again and whatever comes on top he has to add that to the number he arrived at when he added the bottom number. Now for the first time, you turn round and after the very briefest of pauses you tell him what his total was. All you have to do is look at the three faces that are now on the top, add them together and add 7, and that will be the total he is thinking of. Might I suggest that as a further 'put off' you use three differently coloured dice and specify which one he has to pick up and add its bottom face. You would, for example, stress that he must pick up the blue dice and add the bottom face and re-roll that. In this way they will think that although your back is turned that par-

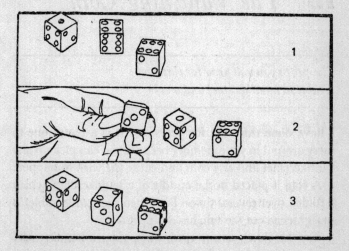

ticular dice has something to do with the trick, and they will be so busy trying to work that one out that they will not arrive at the obvious solution which is, of course, as we all know, that the opposite faces of any dice always add up to 7. So that you really understand this trick let's go through it one more time following the drawings on page 55.

Wisdom Box 6

★★★
★   ★
★   A good general rule is never to tell the audience what   ★
★   you are about to do, because then if it goes wrong   ★
★   you may still be able to perform an alternative trick   ★
★   and the audience will not be aware that something   ★
★   went wrong for you in the middle of the show.   ★
★   ★
★★★

18   *The Vanishing Coin*

The props you will need for this trick:
A table, a handkerchief and a coin

I have done this trick for years and it is a useful one to carry around in your memory because you can pick up any handkerchief and any coin and cause the trick to happen.

A coin is placed in the middle of a handkerchief which is folded over several times. But when the handkerchief is straightened out the coin has disappeared.

Try this slowly as you read. First, place a handkerchief on the table in front of you, with one of the corners facing

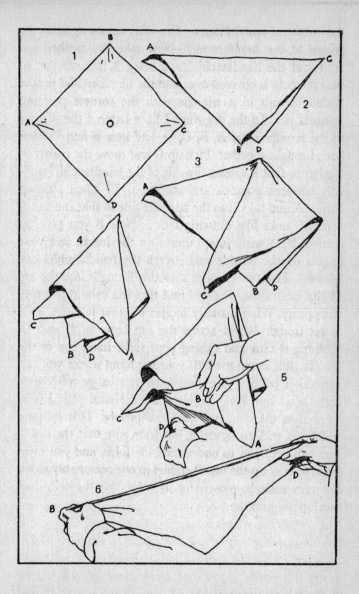

towards your body. Place a coin – any coin – right on the centre of the handkerchief. Now take the farthermost corner of the handkerchief and bring it towards you so that the coin is covered over and the handkerchief is now folded in half in a triangle with the corners pointing towards you. In the drawings I have lettered the corners of the handkerchief A, B, C, D, and now B and D have been brought together. Pick up C and move the corner to the left so that it crosses the side of the handkerchief midway between point A and corners B/D. Then pick up corner A and take it to the opposite side so that the handkerchief looks like drawing No 2. Now if you pick up corners B/D with your thumbs on the inside and your fingers on the outside and stretch the handkerchief out between these two corners, smoothly lifting it into the air at the same time, you will find that the coin apparently disappears. What actually happens is that it 'hides' in a secret trough folded across the top between B and D. Keeping it taut and raising your right hand causes the coin to slide down towards your left hand where you can conceal it behind your fingers as you let go with your right hand and flick the handkerchief with your left to show that the coin has gone completely. This is quite a difficult trick to describe, but I am sure that the drawings will help you to understand the folds, and you must learn to pick up the handkerchief in one reasonably swift, but very smooth, movement in order that the coin does not flip out into the air.

The Vanishing Coin Part 2

You, the wonder-worker, explain that you are going to make a coin disappear under cover of a handkerchief and you display the coin in your left fingertips. The handkerchief is grasped at one corner in your right hand and pulled backwards over the coin; when you have completely pulled the handkerchief clear of your left hand the coin is still there. You are slightly puzzled by this, so you try it again, and it still doesn't go. 'That's a shame,' you say. 'What I wanted to do was cover the coin like so,' and you repeat all the above actions, stroke it with a handkerchief and 'Oh look it's disappeared,' and it has. The person, or persons to whom you are showing this trick will be bewildered and bamboozled. I know I would be if you did it on me.

The first two times you cover and stroke the coin with the handkerchief you are merely getting the audience used to an action. Each time you do it you gaze intently at your left fingers, even though they are covered with the handkerchief, and each time you bring your right hand towards the breast pocket of your jacket as it draws the handkerchief backwards. Now the third time: the audience have seen you fail twice already so won't see any difference in the action when your right hand comes backwards again over the coin, but this time you grip the coin with your right fingers as they travel over it, and this must be done without any hesitation at all. It must be the same smooth

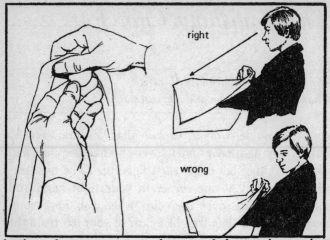

right

wrong

backwards movement you have used the previous twice, and as it comes back all you do (don't forget to gaze at your left fingers) is to drop the coin into your breast pocket. This should happen at the same moment as your left fingers come into view and your right hand then travels away to the side, the coin has disappeared. Used properly this is one of the most effective coin vanishes in magic. So don't waste it, practise it, learn it properly, and you'll probably find that, like me, you'll use it for the rest of your life.

Wisdom Box 7

★★★
★ ★
★ Be sure that you know the trick as well as you pos- ★
★ sibly can before attempting to show it to ANYONE. ★
★ Always strive to make your magic different to every- ★
★ one else's by using unusual props or by devising a ★
★ new method of doing an old trick. The major rule in ★
★ magic is THINK. ★
★ ★
★★★

19 The Label and the Bottle

The props you will need for this trick:
Two identical clear glass lemonade bottles with labels,
newspaper, a pencil, a rubber eraser, blotting paper, a
weight, glue (crystals, seccotine or gum arabic), Blu tack,
a round-headed knitting needle and a pack of cards

You, the Funjuror, stand before your audience – who are, of course, all agog to find out what you are going to be up to next – and you show them a sheet of newspaper and a bottle. This can be any bottle at all that has clear glass, but I prefer to use a large lemonade bottle. You then ask a member of the audience what his or her initials are and you mark the label on the bottle with their initials in pencil, so that they will recognize the bottle should they ever see it again. But that, you say, they may never do, because you are about to perform your world-famous 'vanishing bottle' trick.

You roll up the bottle in a sheet of newspaper and you announce that on the count of three the bottle will disappear completely. '1 – 2 – 3, the bottle has gone' you say, but when you tap it with your wand a very obvious chinking sound is heard. You try it again but it still won't go. In desperation you unwrap the bottle and announce you will have one more try this time with the bottle unwrapped. 'Go' you command, but the bottle just stands there and looks at you. Slowly it dawns on you what is wrong, 'it is your initials, they are putting the bottle off' and you hand

61

the bottle and a rubber eraser to the person whose initials they are and order them to rub the initials off. This they find very difficult to do because somehow the label with their initials on it is now *inside* the bottle and there is no way that they can get at it to rub the initials off. This is one of those tricks that people remember and talk about for a long time after the show.

How do you bring about this amazing miracle? I am glad you asked that, I'll tell you.

You need two identical bottles so that you can soak them and ease off their labels. Having got the labels off the bottles you must then place them between a couple of sheets of blotting paper with a weight on them so that they will dry flat and in good condition. Next you need to mix up a very weak solution of glue. Using glue directly from a bottle does not work because it will be 'too heavy' and show marks on the label that you are going to stick inside the bottle. From a good stationers get some glue crystals, seccotine or gum arabic, and mix up your own solution of glue of a very weak strength. Now when you are going to perform the trick you need to know in advance who is going to be among your audience, whether it be at a party or some other function, so that you can find out a particular name and even then it is best if you can somehow manipulate them to the front of the audience. Of course, if you are working in a small room this doesn't matter very much at all, you can apparently choose your 'victim' at random. Put the initials of your chosen person on to one of the labels which you have trimmed down in size slightly because the curvature of the bottle on the inside is tighter than the outer curve and if you just leave the labels as they are the inside label will go further round the bottle than the outside one. Remember where you have put the initials on the label because you are going to have to mark the exterior label in exactly the same way during the performance.

Now roll up the smaller label that you have initialled and put it inside the bottle, pour in a little of your weak glue solution and, using a round-headed knitting needle, manoeuvre the label into position before tipping out the surplus glue. The label will adhere to the side of the bottle and you then fix the outside label over it. You want to finish up with a bottle looking as though it hasn't been tampered with at all.

pour thin solution of glue into bottle with label

press label in place with knitting needle

paste second label over one inside

finished prop

In fixing the outside label you do it with tiny blobs of wax or Blu tack so that the exterior label can be peeled off easily. During the performance you get the initials and place them on the outside label and wrap up the bottle in the newspaper. When you eventually unwrap the bottle all you do is tear the paper off roughly and while doing so remove the outside label as well and the trick is done.

If you have to entertain at a party, and you do not know who is going to be there, you can, of course, put the name of a playing card on the interior label and during performance put it on the exterior label, and to do this you have to 'force' a card. A nice simple but effective way to do this is to have the 'forced' card on the top of the pack and have the pack cut into two halves by a member of the audience who must then place what was the bottom half of the pack on what was the top half but cross-ways as in the drawing. Then you show the bottle and pencil and say that whichever card he has cut to, that is the one you are going to write on the label. Remove the top half of the pack and pick up the card on top of the lower heap. Because of the slight interval between the cutting and the actual revelation of the card no one will remember that this was the previous top card, and when you show it you then write it on the label. Having marked the label you then continue with the trick as before.

the card is shown face up for clarity — in fact
it is face down on the pack

20 *What a Twist*

The prop you will need for this trick:
A wide elastic band

Here's a funny little trick that you can do any time you happen to come across a wide elastic band, and I do mean wide. You need one of those fat rubber bands that are about a quarter of an inch wide for the trick to be very visual.

You hold the rubber band between right forefinger and thumb, and left forefinger and thumb, as shown in drawing No 1. By sliding the right finger and thumb in opposite directions, as shown by the arrows, you roll the rubber band until you have two twists as shown in drawing No 2. Ask someone to take hold of the rubber band in exactly the same way as you are holding it, in other words you transfer your right finger and thumb grip to his right finger and thumb, and your left finger and thumb to his left finger and thumb, and ask him to see if he can remove the twists from the band by changing the positions of his hands without altering his grip on the two ends. He isn't allowed to roll the band between his fingers, he must merely remove the twists by changing the positions of his hands. He won't be able to do this, so when he is in exactly the same position as when you handed it to him you take the rubber band back, retaining the two twists, so that once again you are holding it as in the second drawing.

Now, lower your right hand and raise your left at the same time, so that your hands pass each other in an up

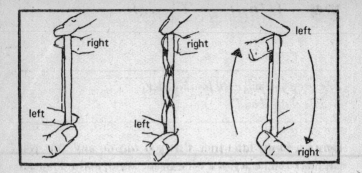

and down movement, and the twists will melt away. Raise your right hand past your left again and the twists will return. Once again hand him the band without losing the twists and once again he will be unable to do this trick. Why? He really isn't getting hold of it in the same way that you are at all. Because he is facing you when he gets hold of the rubber band it is the opposite way on, and there is no way the twists will come out once the rubber band has been gripped in the opposite direction.

21 *Lucky 13*

The props you will need for this trick:
Dominoes

You, the Funjuror, happily chat about the number thirteen, how some superstitious people think of it as unlucky, but you explain that it has always been very lucky for you. As an example you lay out thirteen dominoes, face down in a row, and while your back is turned, or while you are out of the room, someone from your audience moves any number of dominoes from one to twelve from one end of the row to the other, and moves them one at a time.

When you come back, or when you turn round you turn over a domino, and the total of the spots on that domino is exactly the same as the number of dominoes that were moved. This is one trick that you can keep repeating, and probably grows more baffling when you do so.

You will need thirteen dominoes and the spots on their faces must equal the numbers from one to twelve. We have drawn a diagram for you showing a sample lay-out, but of course the dominoes would be laid out face down. The thirteenth domino is a double blank, and so you will lay out your dominoes face down beginning with No 1 from the left, No 2 next to that and so on until the last domino on the right is a double blank.

To show how the dominoes are to be moved you move a few from the left end to the right end one at a time, and before you turn round remember the number of spots on

first lay out (actually face down)

1   2   3   4   5   6   7   8   9   10   11   12   13

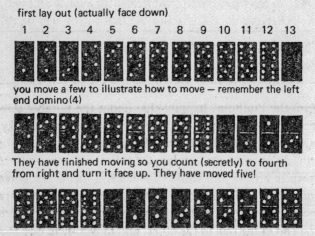

you move a few to illustrate how to move — remember the left
end domino (4)

They have finished moving so you count (secretly) to fourth
from right and turn it face up. They have moved five!

Now count backwards (secretly) to the left end (9) and
remember it for the next go.

the domino on the *left* end. When you come back all you
do is count mentally — that is so that the audience is un-
aware of your counting — to the domino at that number
from the right hand end. For example, if you remembered
the domino on the left added up to seven, you count to the
seventh domino from the right, and when you turn that
domino over it will show the number of dominoes moved.
If the left hand domino is blank you must regard it as
having a total value of thirteen. To repeat the trick all you
have to do is to count from the domino that has been
turned face up to the one on the left hand end and you
can easily work out its value before you turn round again.
If you get one of those clever devils in your audience who
decides to fool you by not moving any of the dominoes

you will find that when you turn your domino over it will be double blank. Should this happen it is quite a good place to stop performing the trick, because it will get a very big reaction and nothing else that you do will be able to 'top it'.

22 *Tubular Magic*

The props you will need for this trick:
Two tubes of different sizes, a metal container with hook on the back edge, items to produce like sweets, handkerchiefs, or streamers

---

The size of this trick is entirely up to you, if you are only little you'll probably only use little tubes, and if you are middle-sized you'll use middle-sized tubes and if you are big you'll use big tubes, and if you are ginormous I won't be able to lift the tubes up for you !

You need to make two tubes, one of which will fit inside the other, the inside tube must be taller than the outside tube. That takes a bit of understanding so have a look at the drawing and you will see exactly what I mean.

I have made these tubes up from time to time using cardboard. I have made square ones using wood, and at other times I have had my mother operate the electric can opener and used two different sized food cans. The advantage of using an electric can opener is that you are not left with any ragged edges.

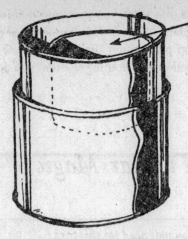

load
chamber

Now for the secret bit that nobody ever sees (if they do you've done the trick wrongly). You need a container with a thin metal hook on the back edge. This container again will depend upon the size of your tubes. It has to have a solid bottom and into this you place whatever it is you wish to produce. Your handkerchiefs, sweets, streamers, etc. When the trick starts the container is hanging inside the tall inner tube with the hook over the back edge away from the audience. Pick up the outer tube taking care not to catch the hook as you come up and show that tube back and forth, put your hands through if it is big enough and do whatever you want to do to prove it is empty.

Point out that it just fits over the tube that is left standing on the table and you demonstrate this by moving it up and down over the inside tube, but in the last upward sweep you engage the hook over the back edge of the outer tube and you pick up the load chamber as you lift this away. Place that tube casually to one side, it is now loaded, and you show the inside tube to be completely empty and replace it on the table. Putting the outside tube back over the inner tube re-hooks the load chamber on to the taller tube and you are all set to make a production of goodies from nowhere.

As with all tricks you must practise this until you can do it very very smoothly. It is a very deceptive way to produce anything and well worth the trouble of making your props.

23 *The Joker is Magic*

The props you will need for this trick:
A pack of cards

The audience sees you look through the pack and place the Joker into your top pocket or stand it to one side. You then deal the cards one at a time on to the table until someone in the audience tells you when to stop. They then see the next card before it is returned to the centre of the pack and the pack is cut several times. Removing the Joker from your pocket you tell them that the Joker will now find your card. You push it into the pack and cut the cards again several times. When the pack is given to a member of the audience he looks through and finds the Joker is right next to the chosen card. To wild cheers and tumultuous applause you take your bow.

Not many card tricks lend themselves easily to a stage presentation, but I think that this is one you could do on any stage or any platform, because although all the audience may not be able to see the trick they can see what is happening, and hear what other members of the audience say when they confirm what has happened.

When you first look through the pack you keep the backs of the cards towards the audience, and move the Joker to the top of the pack. Then you take any card and put it in your top pocket or stand it on display. Deal the cards one at a time face down on to the table until the

audience says stop. Show them the next card without looking at it yourself, and replace it on top of the cards in your hand. Pick up the cards from the table and put them on top of the cards in your hand and you will have placed the Joker next to the chosen card. Cutting the cards will not separate these two unless you manage to bring the Joker to the bottom of the pack. Never let the audience see the bottom of the pack in case this happens at any time during the cutting, but have a quick look to make sure it is not there when you finally take what the audience thinks is the Joker and push it in the pack. Cut the cards again. Again make sure the Joker is not on the bottom of the pack and hand it to someone to look through for the chosen card and the Joker. They will find them together. The Joker is magic !

Index

PAUL DANIELS ADDITIONS TO HIS FABULOUS RANGE OF MAGIC.

Paul Daniels Velvet Range.

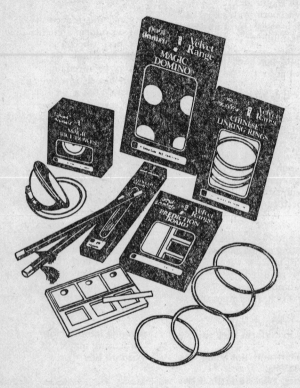

The Velvet range comprises five very special tricks selected by Paul Daniels for this new range, Magic Domino, Chinese Linking Rings, Magic Rice Bowls, Chinese Sticks, Prediction Board.

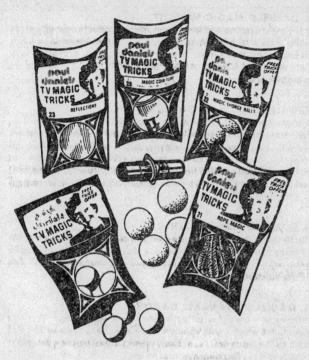

Trick 21, Rope Magic.
Trick 22, Magic Sponge Balls.
Trick 23, Reflections.
Trick 24, Multiplying Balls.
Trick 25, Magic Coin Tube.
Tricks 22 and 24 are the first Black code – Master Magician tricks – offered in the range.

In addition to these fabulous new items the Paul Daniels range of magic now in the shops includes:

PAUL DANIELS MAGIC WALLET
One of the most exciting and impressive magic products ever offered to the public. Paul's 10 brilliant card tricks in a smart, mysterious black wallet. Each trick in its own labelled compartment, complete with profusely illustrated booklet. All 10 Paul Daniels Card Tricks also on sale in individual wallets.

PAUL DANIELS 25 MAGIC TRICKS
All 25 tricks have been performed by top magicians – many on T.V. You can: make objects disappear from your hand . . . predict numbers . . . 'see' a dice number inside a sealed box! . . . push a pencil through solid glass . . . or miniature swords through a 50p coin . . . make a ball escape from a sealed and tied box while your audience watches the ball! An incredible Magic Box makes cards appear, disappear – even change size! – lots more.

PAUL DANIELS MAGIC CARDS
A perfectly 'ordinary' pack of cards – yet you can perform 25 remarkable tricks – many performed by top magicians. You can pull individual cards out of the pack . . . find aces . . . 'read' your volunteer's mind and lots more. Fully illustrated instructions.

PAUL DANIELS SVENGALI CARDS
12 terrific tricks – plus how to 'palm' and do sleight-of-hand. You can actually predict which cards volunteers will choose . . . or a knife point will touch as the cards fall! . . . actually predict a card before a volunteer freely chooses it . . . Dazzling magic at its best.

PAUL DANIELS MARKED DECK CARDS
You can read the back of each card instantly! Write up to four card predictions – before they're chosen! Display amazing feats of memory . . . read volunteers' minds – even when they're outside the room.

PAUL DANIELS MYSTERY BOX
The most remarkable complete magic act ever offered the public. The box looks empty – yet you can take all kinds of things out of it! Put one thing in . . . make it disappear, reappear . . . or even change completely! Eight fabulous tricks: Disappearing Coin Rings, Magic Egg, Spot the Ball, All Seeing Eye, Swords Through Coin, Amazing Escape Ball, Genie in the Bottle, Incredible Magic Drawer. Fully illustrated instructions.

PAUL DANIELS 6 TRICK & 10 TRICK COMPENDIUMS

A complete magic act Paul will show you how to perform really well –
plus advanced techniques like palming and sleight of hand. Either 6 or
10 of Paul's favourite tricks – all performed by top magicians – many on
T.V. A selection from: Mind Reader Dice, Spot the Ball, Sword Through
Coin, Genie in the Bottle, Magic Vanishing Box, Houdini Rings, All
Seeing Eye, Coin Through Glass, Magic Cards, T.V. Magic Card Trick.
Plus: Magic Wand and Booklet. Paul Daniels 50 Magic Tricks.

Paul Daniels range of Magic supplied by: Magic Marketing Limited,
10 Beulah Road, Wimbledon, London SW19 3SB.